screaming at the madness

...and other poems

by alex b. diamond

Cyberwit.net
HIG 45 Kaushambi Kunj, Kalindipuram
Allahabad - 211011 (U.P.) India
http://www.cyberwit.net
Tel: +(91) 9415091004
E-mail: info@cyberwit.net

...for Mom, with love

Contents

a love letter to Daphne and Velma

first of all, I love you!
you girls are such great mystery solvers
akin to private investigators, or
private detectives
that it is a great job, and
a great career!
Scooby-Doo would be a terrible cartoon without you!
this I would like you to know
from the very bottom of
my heart
and
the very essence of my being
my
sophisticated, manly soul, of
handsome, brown-haired love
of
the real female race, the girls
who rock out and
have a dope-ass female life of
doing things that are
fun and cool
you know, living
a life of independent motivation
as if to say
hey, I know I don't have a penis, yet
in between my legs, and
there is a minor flat area there
which makes it seem
like

I don't have a big real human thing going on, yet
but
yo, even so
I like doing things in life
and
I even like to go on and have fun
alone
in my room
in the crib
when I am hanging out
at my crib
and
being a person
who
can have fun all the time
it's fun!
so, to you girls
Daphne, the tall, long-haired one, with
the neck scarf
for fun
and
her best friend Velma
the somewhat portly
generously proportioned one
with the pageboy haircut, and
a nice turtleneck sweater on, year around
I would just like to say
can we hang out sometime
having fun
and
being friends?
and
I already love you!

love is not a hard thing to master, mister

if you love someone
then you shouldn't feel like
they need your love
or something..
you should feel like they
make you happy!
and
make you feel
good
when
they come around...
you love to see them!
you love hanging out with them!
you admire and respect
them
a
lot!
and you know
they are always gonna
be
in your life
no matter how long they might
stay
away for..!
forever!!

purring in the twilight

these silly cats!
they're climbing all over me, Mom!
why
did
you
have
to
get
so many
of them?!
god!
you're crazy, man!
look at this mess!
there's kitties all over the place, man!
geez Louise!
it's like, damn!
kitty-cat mania in this crazy place, man!
meow!
meow!
meow!
that's all I hear, night and day
around
here
man!
I'm gonna go crazy!!

why did I do that when I knew it was wrong?

if you really want to know what the hell is going on
write it in a poem, sing it in a song
I'll tell you this, it's obvious, to those that's in the know
that you feel so excluded, that's why you feel so low
some say it's your ethnicity, but you know it goes much deeper
some say it's your education, and blame it on your teachers
but you know what's really happening to your body and your
brain
you never felt an ounce of joy, you only felt some pain
cause life went by for 20 years, without you even knowing
and now you find it impossible to even get it going
why is it that guys like you are all over the place?
because the only thing you like is a nice body and a pretty face
but life contains much more than that, if you can possibly dig it
first you gotta learn to see with eyes, and not just fidget
they also say your country is the greatest one on earth
and with all this stuff that's going on, it's stable for what it's
worth
what that means is everything just keeps on keepin' on
so don't waste time missing out on the fun your sleeping on
like for instance going to an enjoyable destination
the point of the train is not just to have a subway station
I'm sorry if you're so damn blue that nothing penetrates it
if you wanna know just what to do, you simply have to face it
there is no honey without money, never was, never will be
and if you think the movies are real, now you're just being silly
so, take a walk around the block and then go back upstairs
matter of fact do whatever you want, cause no one really cares

nobody can help you if there's nothing that you want
and all there is around you is some stores and restaurants
so fuck it, sit right on your couch and stare off into space
you know the main problem is you never really had a chance in
the first place
a boring life is nothing new and nothing can really solve it
except maybe earning some money you can deposit
the bottom line is this, you're either living or you're dying
can't fault you for not trying
and I ain't lying...

all I ever wanted was a girl

bitches, man, bitches
so wack!
hoes, man, hoes
all I ever wanted was a freak
not for anything in particular
but because I had nobody good to kick it with
and they sparked my imagination, sluts
so, I rocked it alone
smoking and smoking
working some bullshit
and fucking around
it doesn't matter
I never did no shit you guys ever did ever, I always been differ-
ent
but I don't work no more
yo
no career, no degree, no car, no money, no bank account, no
credit cards, no debit card, no wife, no girlfriend, no kids, no
house, no shit
anyways, I just jack off to sluts now and then
being unemployed
I'm not so strange
I do have a laptop, bitch
and a phone
someone's seeing to it
point is, if nobody teaches me better
cause they're so bitter it's not innate in me
it's their problem
not my fault

anyway, I used to want a woman in my life
now I don't
I'm too unstable right now to face anything
I can't exactly control myself as far as being self-destructive
I admit I need help from a professional
and I need to keep relaxing and pondering my options for as long
as I want, bitch!
I built this world for me to live in freely not just for the fun of
building and feeling like a God you know!
I wanted to have a life, too!
it looks enticing, if you stop fucking squinting all the time!
try this, look in the mirror totally naked
a full length mirror
floor to ceiling
no jewelry
no hair accessories
and just stand there
seems like you're accepting yourself as existing in reality
on earth
in a lifetime, as vulnerable
and having potential
and an identity
full of wonder and opinions
which are okay to have
and express freely
anywhere, anytime
and someone might not like it
and you may be forced to handle that
and that's a responsibility
to keep living
which you realize, you want to do
and that must be good
cause you are full of good

and that's on the right side of things
that's a bit, at least
nobody is nothing
this is all wrong out here
this is all messed up right now
it wasn't always like this
that means things can change
if they can for the worse, then they can for the better
but I need to be scared
this country is chaos
this is madness
man, what a wreck
and then you can think about sex and men and pleasure
and realize that there's fun
and then you think of work
and then you realize oh, buzzkill, there's money
now you're intrigued
big time
money is the root of all evil, not woman
is your first thought
this is all because of man's frustration
with his imperfections, cause it irks his soul
to see such lack of beauty
we are his muses, and his motivators
but we have other ideas about what's important now
we, women, us
wow
demographics matter
anyway, this is all remedial
it's just nice to feel
I'm scared but I'm okay, in fact, I know I'm gonna be safe
no car accidents for me, I know it
long life, no smoking
but I need men

and they're messed up
and imperfect
we are humanity
we ride a star
through space and time
trying to get along, and share what we got
and there's a lotta troublemakers
men are fucking violent cause they don't have an outlet for their
aggression
that's peaceful, cause women haven't stepped up to let the men
beat the shit out of them enough, we tried to tame them by
example
what asshole school marms we are!
that are so weak and puny
anyway
I gotta do something
I want a cigarette and a drink
and I wanna get dressed in some shorts and a t-shirt
and chill out and think and write this down
make some money
content has value
which can be traded for money
boom
best we can do
'til the time is right for the best content ever
which changes our hearts and minds
over to peace
by all means necessary
and then we can live
together
in love with each other
as man and wife
forever
'til death do us part…

my whole game plan was to be immortal

now, you know what I'm saying
time is not a real consideration, but
it's worth mentioning
I haven't given up the ghost yet
I still want things, good things to happen
for me
in the long run
I still feel there's a chance
for
deliverance
for
redemption
why has it taken so long?
this long?
well
it's weird
and
it's complicated, but
things just had to run a certain way
I don't know exactly why
I don't really understand all the forces at work
in my life
in any of our lives
but I do know this
I do know this one thing
light is always gonna be shining through my fingers
and
the written word, the value
of literary expression

can never be
underestimated
when released
with
the power
of
a
gold sparkling
hurricane
this is all I know...

time is an illusion

when I hear the sound of music
I can't even begin to describe what it does for me
man, if you don't know, then you're lost
I love this stuff, right here, right now, and later on, too
okay, I'm gonna share this with ya
when I go off into my own little world
there is no other way to be
because, I can't be captured
it's like a laser gun on my hip
all these people with their petty concerns
start to melt away
like a stick of butter in the microwave
you need to turn that shit up, 'til you can hear it good, real good
and then just sit back and let it wash over you
without worrying about it all the time, man
time doesn't exist
life doesn't exist anymore
these notes are my language
these rhythms are my heart
music
sweet music
come and take over me
conquer my palpitating desires for one or more days
I love you so much, so, so much
you're freakin' cool, man!
ha ha!
yeah!!!

and the Great American Novel is...

called...
'The Road To Los Angeles'
by one John Fante
get it?
like
John Font?
it's about his alter-ego, Arturo Bandini
having to get a job, to support his family, while
still in high school
his mother, his worrisome, flighty mother
and
his prickly, straight-laced sister
he knows he is really a genius, okay, but
he doesn't quite know at what, per se
at some point in the novel, he decides, okay
being a writer
he razzle-dazzles around at various joe jobs, then
after goofing around with them and losing them all
he signs on in a fish processing plant as the only white
among the gaggle of Mexican-Americans
he's diminutive in stature, and has a huge
Ceasar complex, and, hilarity ensues!
it's a laugh riot!
very funny and comical, very
after work he competes a bit with his somewhat brainy, but
more so just disciplined and religious sister
it's really funny
I got an idea for my Great American Chapbook from it...
"pick my brain - sibling rivalry poems"

with a photo of myself and my older sister, the Harvard grad, on
it...
check it out
and here's the magical part
it features some passages about him 'dreaming' about
the pin-ups in his 'artists and models' magazine, if
you catch my drift
so, they wouldn't publish it at the time, in LA!!!
in the 1930s, can you imagine!!
ah ha ha ha ha ha ha ha ha!!
shit...
he kept the lone copy of the manuscript
in a box in the basement of
him and his wife's house, in LA, for over
50 years!
and then, well
it was finally published, when Charles Bukowski finally
got up the cojones to ask to meet him, in the
early 1990s...
artists and models!
okay, Fante, okay, you dirty dog!
we see you, buddy-roo!
ah ha ha ha ha ha ha ha ha!!!!

once when I was thirteen

my step-ma yelled at
me
for nothing
on
a bright sunny day
so
I went into my bedroom
and
turned out the light
closed the blinds
and
started sulking
hoping
she would notice
it would've went a little like this
hey, baby
what's wrong?
why are you sitting here
inside?
it's nice out!
why you don't go out and
play?
I don't feel like it!
now
leave me alone!
was it something I did?
I said
I don't wanna talk about it!
now, please, just

leave me alone!
go away!
okay
okay
I'm sorry I disturbed you
hey
you''re not gonna do anything to
harm
yourself, are you?
fuck off!
leave me alone!
I said
I'm fine!
just
go
away!
okay, I see
well
you
have a right
to
your
feelings
I'll
leave
you
alone
if you wanna talk about it, I'm
here
get
the
fuck
out!

I just wanna be left
alone!
okay?
is that okay? or
not?
please?!
okay
I'm
sorry..
dinner will be ready around 6:00
I don't care!
go away!
okay
that's fine
sorry I disturbed you
whatever!!
hm
okay
love you!
shut up!!

music and me

I love all kinds of music
funk
new wave
classic rock
house
jazz-funk
reggae
50's rock 'n roll
blues
rap/hip hop
that's about it
I don't like
metal
country
or hardcore/punk
I feel quite lucky, and much gratitude for it all
I really do
George Clinton of Parliament-Funkadelic, is an uber-genius
Bob Marley as well
The Cure is no joke
New Order is amazing
Depeche Mode is my heart
there's too many great rappers and rap groups to list, many
great albums, at least about 50, all told
real albums, not pop, you know, good
all the way through, every song
but I must say, I really, really love
Ministry
the album "Twitch" is such a masterpiece it's

practically
unfathomable
I'm sure glad I speak English!

the ballad of a night angel

you're so supple and
sweet
to me
you really don't know how high I get
when we meet to pet
ha ha
oh yes, oh yes
you're like a rainbow flower
and I need you
I need you
never stray, and leave without a
trace
I love your face
maybe I don't look at you, and
know what you're all about, as it were, okay
but
that's not in my blood
and, well, I don't really care, cause
I can't really even fathom your elegant proportions
like that
but, listen
I do love you
babe
I really do
and
that's forever...

an Arab in the west

well, technically. I'm really a Jew
Jew
funny word, that
but, anyway
yeah
it's weird having Arabs in
the west..
we're not exactly, you know
swingin'
drinkin'
dancin'
party-time
folk
ha ha
we're Middle Eastern
ancient societies
the Fertile Crescent
pharaohs and sultans
the pyramids
the Sphinx..
but
I'm
a poet
yes
I
am!

anger is a drug

absolute necessity
determines that we eat
forgetting about the past happens
daily
but, hey!
there's more to the picture than meets the eye!
yes
contradictions are often fought out in the media
but, how can you tell who's lying?
and who, if anyone, is telling the truth?
well, common sense helps
look at the big picture
look at the last 150 years, and compare and contrast
the voices you hear
with
what seems logical to happen
and
what seems likely to happen
and
what makes sense
but
stick to your guns
when debating
so
you can see it through to the end
force out
an
opinion
even

if you don't care
so the children won't get scared
that
it's all for naught
and try
try
to
remain calm
don't fly off the handle, man
it's not so serious
some people, man
they do that all the time, cause
it
feels
good
but
it's very immature
to get that mad
at anyone
try not to do that anymore
people of earth
this is paramount
anger is a drug
which is a flaw in our physiology
it
actually
feels
great
especially
afterwards
but, like all narcotics
it's dangerous to over indulge in
this is clear

so, be alright, my people
and
don't
fuck
up
ever
again!!!

so, be alright, my people
and
don't
fuck
up
ever
again!!!

what the fuck does suckiness have to do with anything?

I mean, I'm 47 years old!
I'll be incredibly lucky if I live to just 77!
since I been a pack a day smoker since I was 14
I am deathly afraid of cancer
lung cancer, or worse, brain cancer
fuck
of course, right now, I am out of money
flat broke, so, I can't buy any cigarettes
I swear up and down on a stack of fifty bibles
I'm gonna try and make it stick this time
I think I can do it, I really do
Farley just knocked on my door and gave me four cigarettes
Newport longs
but, fuck it, man!
fuck it, I say!
I gotta do it, I gotta quit!
life is a bag of shit sometimes, man
I live in this nursing home for the insane, MADO it's called
just about everybody here is completely normal, though
they really should be having jobs, and taking care of themselves
not scamming disability
I am one of those
almost everybody, I say, cause there are a few weirdos
there's a youngish guy, Chris, who is white and pudgy and looks
like a giant potato
he talks to himself all day long, constantly asks me for cigarettes,
and

hasn't bathed in months, maybe longer
his room smells awful when I walk by
he has a girlfriend, this lady from India, or maybe Pakistan, who
has bleached blonde hair
and follows behind him all day, as he paces on the patio, mum-
bling to himself
there's another youngish guy, Steve, who's Chinese, who used to
talk to
himself continually, but has stopped
and I mean, he used to talk to himself LOUD
not raving or anything, I mean, it seemed conversational
it was just loud as hell, and he'd be going on like he was talking
to someone
always saying, like, okay, you know what I mean, and have you
ever heard of such-and-such
well, the thing about them is, and you need to know one important
thing
about them, etc, etc
but, he stopped
I don't know if they changed his meds, or what
he also quit smoking
he never eats the cafeteria food, his parents bring him
homemade Chinese food every night
then there's this guy Donnell
he's probably in the worst shape of anyone here
he's a black dude, over fifty, he never talks, but
he carries around two or three transistor radios
with himself at all times, and he flips through the stations, or
sometimes he just pays fuzz and static
he drops them all the time and they seem to break, but he always
has them working
he's into fabric, and what I mean by that is, he cuts up clothes
and ties the strips of them

around his leg or his head
he also frequently wears mismatched shoes, and also carries
extra shoes with him
in plastic bags
he never leaves the premises, but he's not the only one
there's about a good ten or so folks here, maybe 15, men and
women here, that never speak
and never seem to do anything except come down for meals, and
then go right back up to their rooms
stay there all day, everyday
that's the saddest part
I mean, it's bad enough that there's all these old people here that
are clearly gonna die here
but, like I said, there's all these folks that do nothing but lie
around in their rooms all day
I don't feel like going on further, and I don't know what the point
of this poem is
except to say
life here at MADO pretty much sucks
and
I'm really gonna try to quit smoking!

lost stuck in the comfort zone

be careful!
be careful!
feel the vibe, see the vibe
like us balding mothafuckas do
I can see over continents
the Rothschild family's compound is over in Argentina
on the eastern side, bleeding over a sliver
into
Brazil
wait, time out!
Brazil?!
boom-boom contest time!
and go!!
da da da da diddy da da da diddy diddy da da da da
wee yoo wee yoo wee yoo weeeeyow!
damn, baby!
I mean, fer real! damn!
damn
you are so damn fine!
it's like, fuuuuuuuuuck!
fuck it, I love you, fuck it
do you want a hug, baby?
yes, I do want a hug, yes, but in the moment, can you
press your tits against me?
mmmmm....
nice
damn
it's kinda sad, cause, like, there's too many!
how can I love them all!?

or even make a dent?
damn
anyways
oh well!
well, see ya!
hey, maybe we can stay in touch, this
don't have to be the end!
your last Al D. experience!
email me your number on my professional website
Al.com
jog my memory about our tryst, and
we can jaw down!
I'd love to holla at ya again, baby!
you're awesome!
boom boom?
yes
boom boom
damn...

Pan Am flies to 250 destinations nationwide

Washington, DC is greasy
Chicago is hollow
New York has a few dorks
Dallas is a palace
Houston is confusin'
Boston is high costin'
San Francisco is pissed, though
Seattle is addled
Detroit is worse than Beloit
Miami is up for a Grammy
Atlanta still believes in Santa
Philadelphia has gonorrhea
Milwaukee is too cocky
Oakland must be jokin'
Los Angeles is super scandalous
San Diego is out of potatoes
St. Louis used to be all Jewish
Minneapolis is predominantly soulless
New Orleans is for orphans
Las Vegas has no basis
Phoenix needs a Kleenex
Austin is just plain rotten
Omaha misses Obama
Newark is just a bulwark
Cleveland is hardly breathin'
Indianapolis is ridiculous
Denver has bad weather
Memphis is fucking endless
Nashville is full of assholes...

when I was happy

if you think all people suck
you suck
if you think everybody is bad
you are wrong
if you think you are the only person on earth
you are not
if you think you can make life work
you can
but
if you don't try
you won't win
and if you don't win
you won't be alive to see the victory of your soul
but
it doesn't really matter
does it?
yes
it does
everything makes a difference in your life
everything in your world is not yours
but
you can have as much as you can get
nobody cares if you are not perfect
man is the great person here
don't follow?
never mind
I wasn't talking to you anyway
you are too thick to listen
and too cold to care

and too dumb to understand
anyway
and
too
fucked to
bother with
puny human
you are lost in space
and
you are now not ever gonna find your way, unless
and only unless
you
obey
your
heart
obey
your
heart…

a requiem for the porn star, Allie Poison, in three parts

oh, lawd, why lawd?
did Allie have to suffer so?
she was a good kid, lawd!
so blonde!
so fair and blue-grey eyed, lawd!
how pretty like the Earth marble at
daybreak she was, my lawd!!
oh!!
now, the darkness has passed for this indigent
blessed soul of
unfortunate glory, my shepherd!
the flock will follow, if you
lead us to the righteous path, my supple savior, lawd!
we need you now, more than ever, my grace!
please help us
understand the scope and spectrum of mankind's
inordinate evil and
self-hatred
scorn, and
recalcitrance, lawd!
if you don't do something soon
then through the justice of
collective guilt
we will all be fried on
the cross of
mortal weakness, lawd!
please assist us in trying to
rid the community of the

supple, purple stain of
velvet cloth fabric and a
white lace veil and
the first
feeling of a
new spring or winter, lawd!
and also, we pray for
our peace officers, who
are so familiantly weak, lawd!
they are so over-burdened
with so much heinous crime in
these days and times that
they are almost literally driven to tears, lawd!
driven to the point
of straight weeping, your grace!
real big, beefy, strong-armed
beefcake-looking cops of the
big urban city are crying and
weeping real tears, and
the tears are streaming down their rosy
cherubic cheeks, lawd!
please help us, and them,
those poor cops, lawd!!

AMEN

please pass this message on to the president

eclipse this
if you please
I know myself
I know
who I am
I don't make mistakes
I don't try heroin
I do things for my own
fun
my own
enjoyment
not to force
a
consistent
identity as a
reliably me, me
fuck that shit, you phony
try to get your head right
that is, sane!
and then
enjoy life
with..?

crazy shit is the ultimate aphrodisiac

we're clowning here all the time
nobody knows exactly what it's like
or how it all works
then they get sadly scared
and then shocked and dismayed
a moment of righteous outrage
which some try to grow and spread
you'd assume
then somebody else exploits the catastrophe for money
it doesn't sell copies
so, then they shrug their shoulders and say
ball's in your court, we're buffaloed
concerned to the extreme, you might say, distraught over the
situation even
then
holy war
end times fantasies
from the yahoo element
the test is how can the establishment clean up
this mess without making money off it
they feel they always have to make money off it
or the country will collapse
this problem is far too grave and serious
and their a little perplexed and slow to respond
they sell it as cautious, but really, they're not sure what all to do
so, the problem reaches an apex and begin to go down
just as a fact of time passing
they study how that happened
and try to formulate an all out plan

the people have almost no input
for one, they are all bogged down in extremism
and aren't being realistic
second, they're hurting too much to think clearly
plus the political element is paranoid, the activist element
is not effective, they're pushing when the establishment is
already trying as hard as it can
so, what happens is either a leader emerges
and takes control of the whole movement
or the people stage a revolution
which can be bloody and violent
or can be political in nature
but whatever happens
the establishment believes they will remain
and in two scenarios they don't
in armed revolution, they all die
in the political revolution
they survive to observe from abroad living in some degree of
wealth
less than they had here presumably
if the revolution is successful they always solve the major
problem
the question is can they run a functioning society
from then on
and the world allow that once
the former establishment is out there and they're power is
dispersed
in the world at large
coalescing in culturally friendly areas
across the globe at large…

how to end racism

black history classes
as well as
black literature-very important!!!
integrated grade schools
leading
to
diverse social circles
black friends, Hispanic friends, Asian friends
female friends
nerdy friends
and
dirty friends
a rich friend always pays off to have
but
most importantly
critical and
crucial is
for
white teens to have some
true
black friends
guys
you can not be
sane
or
smart
about America
until you do...

screaming at the madness

revolt!
revolt, I say!
forsooth, it is the only path forward!
hark!
hark!
death to the doomsday profiteers!
the ignoble bellyaching of mankind is defeated!
now we know how to deal with it!
victory is ours, and the new adventures of
us can be launched!

I like munching, cause food is good!

yum!
this food is good!
eating is the bomb-diggy, if
you ask me, Mom!!!
yum!!
can I have some more, please?
listen up!
if eating is wrong, I don't even wanna be
right, ya follow?
I'll just go on ahead and
be wrong instead, Mom!
word!
I love it!
look
do you notice how I keep
manipulating these utensils
to shovel grub in
my
gullet?
at a mile a minute, it's so
good?
look!
are you watching?
food eating is right up
my alley, god damn it!
I think I'mma keep doing it
forever!
what do you think, Mom?
yay!

barefoot in Bulgaria

I never left this land, and if I did
I'd not return
the level of hate and stupidity here is enough
to make me never come back
Americans are idiots
if you're a radical, they say get a job
if you're a liberal they say you hate your country
if you're an artist they say you're crazy
if you're a weed smoker, they say you have brain damage
if you're a cop they say you're a hero
if you're a soldier or veteran they say you should be worshipped,
and
that your sacrifice should never be forgotten, while
they leave you homeless in the street
and suicidal from PTSD
then vote for scumbags who underfund the VA
and
housing initiatives
and mental health programs
too
I've been all over
I've been to Chicago and New York City and Los Angeles
and San Francisco and New Orleans and Washington DC
and Milwaukee
and Baltimore
and San Diego
and Indianapolis
and Atlanta
and Boston

New Orleans was the best, though
there was beer, dancing, and titties in the streets
I can follow that, you know?
that makes sense
life should be a party!
work hard! is all you hear
if you work really hard, you can achieve your dream
I never had any dreams
I like smoking cigarettes
and weed
I like pizza, and bacon and sausage and pork chops
I like music the most though
me and my uncle have that in common
I'd like to live in Jamaica
or Belize
they speak English in Belize, I could make it there
cause America is for the birds, man
trust me, it sucks
don't move here if you were thinking about it
that'd be a mistake
morons run everything
morons and haters and lame-asses
the shitheads in charge and the dimwits who voted for them
racism abounds
they say there's a lot of anti-semitism here too
although I never experienced any
but
truth be told, I am hesitant when people ask me what I am
to say I'm Jewish
what are you?
ever since grade school, from the job to the mental hospital to the
jail house
what are you?

what are you?
you probably don't hear that anywhere else in the world
people know what you are, you're Jamaican
you're Belizean
or
Brazillian
or just
happy
they should name a country Happistan
that'd be a funny happenstance
I guess my dream is just to keep dreaming, basically
dream about living in a country where there's justice
and
equality
and
safety, safe streets, peaceful cities, not rampant
unceasing
violence and murder, every day very week every month every
corner
of
the country
they always fixate on Chicago but there's heinous violence
everywhere
in America, everywhere
it's psycho
truly
just nuts
the experiment failed
freedom except for slavery turned out to be not so solid a foun-
dation
not so rational a concept
this place is doomed
and, one day, one fine day

you won't see me, or it, anymore
if you see me?
the poet of this pen?
you will see me as a growing person
you don't grow here
you ever notice that?
we don't grow as life goes on here
really
if you see me though?
one wonderful day
I will be be
barefoot
on
the
beach
in
Belize
free
free at last
free at last
thank God all mighty
I escaped America!!!
nice…

fuck these major songs of the canon, if they're just out to make money off our problems for bands, man

solo artist are way better than bands
bands get distracted by the name
some band names are too good, others are comically bad
a good one is
Black Sabbath
and
Motley Crue
and
Minor Threat
and
Public Enemy
and
Talking Heads
and
not
Jefferson Airplane, or
Credence Clearwater Revival
but
John Fogarty is a solid rock musician, so it was a plan, ok?
the best solo artist as a name for a music act
has got to be
Otis Redding
cause that's, like, unique, and he's unique, and far-reaching into
the future
unique, cause you don't know anyone named Otis
or
Redding, right?

no, not in Chicago, not for sure in that sweet hometown
and all you know in the South is
some bullshit like
Gumby and Pokey
the rubber donkeys
nobody down there knows Agnostic Front
and
Rights of the Accused
guarantee that...

does anyone give a shit about being a man?

anyone?
like, say, oh, I don't know
Sammy Sosa?
does anybody in the entire nation
actually care about, and really explore
just being a man?
And think about it, like a human should?
and, you know
show some game
don't let what some other goofy motherfucker
say
be your mantra
for
being a man, son!
define it for yourself
as for me
well, one
a man is not a woman
or an animal
a man
is not a boy anymore, either
or
a punk
or
a pussy
or
a slave
a man
is

free
for real, though
he does whatever he truly wants
to do
all day, and
maybe all night, too
what he truly wants to do, but
within some reason
nothing unsafe for him
like, oh, say, shooting a motherfucker and
going to prison
like a total asshole!
no
he does what he wants
and
also
importantly
nothing
he doesn't
want to do
then, there's more—
he patrols his hood
and
earns a ruthless reputation
for severe violence
so no other man dares
fuck
with his hood
and, okay, here's why
so that
his women and children
can go out
and

shop and play
safely
on
their own...

a poem for this girl named Jackie Bailey

oh girl, you are so blonde
did you know that many blonde girls are considered very hot?
I like the way you look
as far as being interested in saying
you're pretty
Jesus Christ, I feel so embarrassed
to announce that to you right now
why don't you tell me what you feel
when I compliment you as being a girl
who's combination of blonde hair
and the way your face looks
equals
you are very pretty
and I want to be the one to tell you that
so, you know, I can stop hiding it
that it is very nice for me to see
when I see you around me in town
I really like it when that happens to me
in fact, I think I will definitely remember you
the rest of my life
matter of fact
I really know I will always remember you
how pretty you looked
and your memorable name
Jackie Bailey
the blonde girl
          who's dope…

internet riot

I can steal your identity
send it to me
I can take your mind
and meld it with mine
I can take your i-phone
hack into it from my home
I can take what's in your head
and put it on the worldwide web
technology
won't set you free
society
will exploit it
can't avoid it
can't destroy it
it's our fate
it's too late
too deny it…
it's an internet riot!
I can steal your info
by looking in your window
but why should I bother
when you're life's online
and you're the author?
you want fame
for your name
so you play the game
it's all so lame
completely tame
a crying shame

you're all the same
don't deny it
you came
to start an internet riot!

I hate little girls, man

hey, Bob
yeah, Skippy?
you ever notice there's these damn little girls
everywhere?
oh yeah. pisses me off. big time
yep. gonna have to make a plan, us men of Paperonia
probably another torture laden genocide
if I can't get some peace and quiet
from
all that hellified giggling and
gum-snapping
real bad news, Sargent Gun
oh yeah. Victor Charlie girl war time, this June
I know it, I know it
pass me a Budweiser beer, my friend
sure, buddy, no problem, I have a whole Igloo full of
them, in brown bottles for us to sip slowly and be very
macho and relaxed, wearing jeans, and sitting in the
sunset, buddy...here, catch!
thanks, homie. that's polite talk we as men invented
in the 1600s, the European Renaissance Hunting Days
I was there
painting frescos
I'm over 538 years old. big time man. real person here
but, back to the war, work, art at hand, these
goddamned ubiquitous little girls all over
the twin cities are just out of control, Steven!
oh yeah, Jacob Rosenstein, I agree! I really, really, really do!
let's see if we can't dial up Mr. Teddy Freddyson

from North Englandberg and
get that new laser invention rented, or leased
and fire guns at the problem
for a while, cause
the women need yarn to keep knitting
in
their Pilgrim bonnets, our dicks are super hard and
horny for blonde babes of the Los Angeles taco truck
people, and plus, and listen
this is the kicker
we need fireworks for our
pride and victory celebration, plus the right
permits and huge money banks to get crazy
with the junk mail industry, and all our
digital watches, for the poor, and
silver watches for us Republican business winners, too
'yawn' excuse me, I was getting tired, 'burp'
excuse you! that was rude!
sorry, I flunked out of the Marines
anyway
just a few more brontosaurus burgers with A-1 steak sauce
or Miracle Whip, and
we'll be ready, it's war!
death to little girls!
ooh-rah!!!
what I think Dr. King should've done..

all that meshugana of the '60's
seems totally unnecessary, to this poet, me..
here's what I would've done..
just arrange for Dr. King, and one of those
bag of shit hate-filled Southern senators, say
Senator Strom Thurmond, and even, yes, a

member of the Ku Klux Klan, any one
get together with Walter Kronkite
live, on CBS, nationwide
and
sit around a round table, calmly, and
calmly discuss the white racism problem
for hours and hours
as necessary
no Freedom Riders
getting killed, like poor
James Chaney, and poor old
Michael Schwermer, and the great activist
Andrew Goodman, who all knew
they were gonna die...
may all three
find
eternal
bliss
in
paradise...
that's what
I
would've done...

it's a bird, it's a plane, it's an alien, it's an Italian

this poem must be very respectful
this intro is not the start yet, so, wait…
so, watch the way you eat cheese and sun-dried tomatoes
feta crumble is nice, I mean, listen, listen guys, come on
I like it, I drizzle some nice vinaigrette oil on
the mozzarella and chive butter fried pitas
with garlic, sprinkle on the bacon bits, the nice kind, the thick
ones, okay
and that's a good snack for the brunch hour
around say, oh, the 11:30 news edition
with that nice local girl from the west side
the cable box store magnate, Fonzi, what's
that nice girl's name, on the news?
the one who smokes Salem Lights 100s
on the side as a hobby? Ted DuBrose's daughter?
Bethany DuMayne, channel 12
correct, exactly, she's adorable!
I'm impressed, cause she's happy as a clam crumble
she loves her life here, two or three twin daughters
and
honestly? it makes me proud
that we, the Italians of Greater Vancouver
built this entire major metropolis, this
whole city, in the '80s…

nerds nerds nerds nerds nerds

ooh wow look here a damn antique store!
whoa!
damn!
wow!
this this is living man
can you believe we used to live in Lombard and now
we got all this
I mean, there must be four antique stores around here!
plus, and this you'll never believe
a cafe
where they have coffee
and, and, and
you can sit there and fuck around on your laptop!
they even let you!
thank god we got out of Lombard and
are now in an area with at least
four, count 'em, four antique stores!
I'm gonna buy a whole gang of antiques, baby!
lamps
end tables
shelves
more lamps
holy moly roly poly
my stupid mother is still in Lombard
and she doesn't even live in an area with
so many little antique stores like me, Brian
wow
this area is really hoppin' and boppin', antiques wise
I must say
so cool!

an ode to Nintendo

Princess Peach, I'm coming to your rescue!
before the Koopa troopers get you
bopping bricks, leaping pipes
I'm doing it all for women's rights
I'm Underground, straight out the sewer
swimming in poison, no one is truer!
I'm Mario baby, say my name
I'm the star of this game, I get all the fame
but you're my heart, the point of the story
without you, there is no glory
ultimately, girl, you're what it's all about
World 8-4, the hidden route
without you I'd lack soul, crunch, any texture
if you were ugly, some poor fat heifer
I jump and run and shout and fly
all because you get me high
I wanna play, I'm bored at home
I just didn't want a pre-fab adventure
only to make one silly poem!

Mike Jenkins is not my friend

he
doesn't
understand me
and
he always
thinks the worst about
my
intentions
ignoring the obvious
fact
that I am a
wonderful, and very nice
very loving
person
to one
and
all!

.

the Messiah speaks in verse

I know
life is hard
when there's a conspiracy afoot
people act weird, cause they're pretending
people just keep on walking, keep on driving
all damn day there's cars
swishing by down Ashland outside my window
from 6 am to midnight
I actually can't figure out how
people can drive around all day
in new model cars
during working hours
and
incessantly
where do they get the money?
and why are they so lame?
I can't afford a bus fare
three bucks
but
life is good!
life is good, and getting better all the time
I'm blossoming!
poet
photog
artist
singing musician, and dj
comic, comedian, I write comedy too
it's rather uncanny
exactly how many talents I have, thank you

something
big
had to happen, to
produce a man like me, here
everybody is confused
everybody is unsure, stepping lightly
and not seeming to be
too happy
it's evident there's a shit-ton of dumbfucks around too
I hear their stories on the news
they call cops on kids' lemonade stands
for lacking a permit
like
amazing
assholes
particularly that it's done on a racial pretext
there's
big
fucking
assholes
all over
the place
in my land
women too
women too
this displeases the Messiah!
greatly!
the savior hates racism!
he
is
so
indebted
to the

black race
as a huge
colossal
music lover
music fiend
hip hop brainiac
funk junkie
house head
blues aficionado
and
reggae lover
that it makes me NAUSEOUS
the way so many stupid, brutish, worthless white people abuse
abuse them!
after all they've suffered already
after all they contributed
to MY COUNTRY
music
literature
fashion and slang
sports
dance
inventions
and, most holy
freedom fighters!
political radicals at the cutting edge of expanding rights, and
justice, and freedom
black people built America
uncompensated!
and whipped
raped
maimed
kept in ignorance

separated from their loved ones on a whim
their babies ripped out of their loving arms
and sold like a piece of meat
never to be heard from again
and now white people want to criticize them?
judge and castigate them
for grievances
they
have?!
it's so absurd
that it's beyond an insult
to my intelligence
it's an insult to
the intelligence of
a
toddler
this displeases the Messiah greatly!
he is not just ordained, and fated to be the holy savior
he is a mortal man
with natural feelings
and a psyche
that
is
nice!
I
don't
like
hurting
people,
man!
it
makes
me

feel
bad!
I don't want to be a bad guy
or
a hell raiser
or
a gangster
in
any
way
shape
form
or
fashion
I'm a caring man, a
good man
and—
if you MONSTERS
EVER
get a taste of justice for your trampling of human beings
innocent of offense, displaced and cut off from
their culture
their language
their land
their ways
their God
their history
essentially, ghost
human beings
it
will
be
a

great
day
indeed!
this would make the Messiah overjoyed
cause you guys are a bunch of assholes, man
and all
all
all
the shit you spew
sounds
so
fucking
stupid
to
us
good people
that you are simply making a GIANT ASS and a GIANT FOOL
of yourselves!
this does NOT please the Messiah, as a way to look down on
people
and laugh at them and feel superior over them
the Messiah doesn't work that way
he has
no ego
no low self-esteem issues, flipped
into overcompensating by claiming superiority
you work that way
not the Messiah!
the Messiah has pride
and
dignity!
you know, dignity?
look it up

he is plainly and truly
happy
to be himself
Al Diamond
the Messiah
of the human race
the savior
sent by God
a good looking guy
tall
thin
handsome
stylish
nice
woke
and
talented
I don't have a dollar
but I'm glad to be me!
wouldn't you be?
I am happy
because, I like being me
and
I behave
easily
I am not
racist
sexist
homophobic
xenophobic
I don't hate my fellow man, man!
like an asshole!
that's a direct route to unhappiness you bozo-clown!

are you some kind of caveman?
cause if you are, hey
that's no excuse
the Messiah doesn't accept excuses
neither does life
the Messiah likes his lot in life
and
his future looks downright luminescent!
I am blessed
I am getting all the blessings you dimwits forego
for racism
fools
utter
assclowns
is what millions of you are
this makes the Messiah say, what the hell is wrong with you
people?
why are you so fucked up?
aren't you glad and feeling lucky to be an American?
you moron?
aren't you glad you're free?
and
in a high standard of living nation?
you
pig
you
spoiled
greedy
hateful
ignorant
foolish
mean
ugly

pigs!
fuck you!
change, or be castigated
to hell!
the Messiah has spoken!
word!

Hector, the defector

Hector was this homeless guy
I befriended when I
was living up in Andersonville
it started out with me bumming him a few
cigarettes
and me giving him
$2 here and there
as he sat
and
panhandled
in front of the McDonalds
right by my crib
he would go out there at 7 in the morning
and beg all day
until 6 or 7 at night
pretty soon after I met him, I invited him up to
my crib to smoke some weed
he lived under an awning, in a parking lot
of a closed-down Carson's Ribs
up on Ridge and Peterson
by the White Castle
he had a big tricycle, with a
trailer thing attached to it
anyway
all he did was panhandle all day
and
spend the money he made on crack rocks
$20 rocks, which he would get
for

$17, or $18 all the time
when we first started hanging out, I
would let him use my phone to call
his dealers
Blue
G Money
Big Homie
and others
I didn't smoke with him
I was just into weed at the time
and
I was wary of doing crack, because I
had been through that, in the '90s
and
I had experienced the jonesing for more, which
makes you sell off all your belongings, and
I didn't want to go through that again
he used to come rushing up to my crib
seconds before having to shit so bad he couldn't hold it
anymore
sometimes it was too late, and
he shit his pants
anyway, soon after we started kicking it
I didn't feel right letting him
leave my crib late at night
and
go out to sleep in the cold and snow
so, I let him live with me
he taught me about picking up snipes
off the ground
snipes are half-smoked cigarettes
that bar goers, and club goers, and restaurant goers
throw away

living with him wasn't too bad, but
there was some drawbacks
main one being, he was a dumb ignorant redneck
and
had
all
the expected redneck faults:
he was racist, and used the N-word regularly
then, when called on it, deny he was racist
and say some stupid shit
that the n-word just meant ignorant, not black
I pointed out that he only used it
about black guys, when he thought they
were being ignorant, and making him mad
he also hated Mexicans
and gays
and foreigners
and blah blah blah
he used to fart and go—uh oh!
every fucking time
couldn't just say excuse me
the idiot
he also didn't know how to spell his own name
his name, Hector Lopez, was
some fake shit anyway
he was just pretending to be Hispanic
it was a crock of shit
his real name was Richard Grant
he was from the deep south
Huntsville, Alabama
he told me a few stories
like, he once defended a little black girl that three Klan members
were about to kill

bullshit
then he said he served thirteen years in the army
and strangled three Iraqis to death with his bare hands
all bullshit
then he said he had spent time in New York
working for the mob
wearing a suit, and repossessing businesses
total crap, lies
then he said he spent time in Pelican Bay, and
had been a Latin King there
bullshit, garbage
all gang members have gang tattoos
all he had was this stupid devil head, and
this lame Yosemite Sam tattoo
which, he claimed he did himself, left-handed
lies
anyway
eventually I started smoking crack with him
and, well, long story short
I had to stop walking around the hood up there with him, cause
every time a couple guys passed us, he would yell
'it's Adam and Eve, not Adam and Steve!' at them
like a total dipshit
he's an idiot, and I'm glad he's back homeless again, and now
nobody gives him spare change, or dollars anymore
for whatever reason
he sits out there all day still, though, like an idiot
for
nothing
a waste
of
sperm and
egg…

why do you act like a dick, fucker?

you like problems?
you like watching people feel bad because of you...why again?
you like hating, and being hated...cause...why, now?
never heard of good times?
too stupid to avoid trouble? bad is good?
what
that makes you feel smart, or something like that?
that's smart to you? up is really down?
good is really bad?
pain is really pleasure?
being a shithead to people is fun, cause, as a skinny, weak
nobody
it's hilarious that you can actually effect other people at all?
cause...why again?
you lack any morality or respect for humanity, which includes
yourself
you know..?
you're so spoiled, and your life has been so easy
to survive, if not enjoy, that
you strut through town just shitting on good people, like
so you can giggle at watching them suffer?
and you suppose that's gonna last?
you suppose you're safe forever?
which shouldn't even matter
it's obvious to be nice to people...
it's quite fun, and really feels good
so, you're just an abject monster inside?
looking for trouble?
a spoiled brat?

your parents raised you up to be a shit?
and, you don't even care if you get comeuppance and punish-
ment?
suffering?
that's how dumb and completely subnormal you are?
okay
well, you're gonna get crippled
by us
and you will starve and die of thirst
if
no one takes pity on you
and
takes care of you
which, they won't
if you just spit on them
when they are changing your shitty diaper, you know?
okay, so your plan is just to double down and
be completely
incorrigible about it, then?
that's what you want to do with your life, idiot?
okay, idiot
that's what you will try
and
we ill do as we wish to you
which will
be
ill...

somebody yelling cryptic bellows in the moon glow, just for me

if all of my yearnings are not apparent, tonight
it's not like you need to panic, or
something
just give it a little extra time!
maybe a few more nights, or so
things will probably clear up, and
begin to come into view, to come into focus
probably they will, yeah
it's more than likely, yeah
cause, the main thing to realize, is
everybody
is not, like
some kind of prop
some kind of pop, or mama on a mission
we are still, all just..
potential moon glow!
and.
cinders on an ash pile
that has yet
to
respect us the fire, and spark!!

forces are aligned against us, but we main-
tain

all of the reasons for

encroachment are apparent

and we will burn with emotion

before tomorrow

please release this word of rotten scorn

for all we are and all we could ever

desire is right before us

laid out in gold and chocolate

for our feast of the new horizon

on the rise...

Boo-Berry is the best cereal, but Count Chocula is the breakfast for kids bomb, yo!

I like milk, okay?
let's get that straight from jump
so, the cows are doing a good job, don't
end them! plus
God would be pissed!
okay, the
reason Boo-Berry is so good, is cause it's not, for one
Frankenberry
Senator Al Franken is a disgrace to
the Democratic Party due to his
rampant Baby Boomer-ism
hairy-type stuff
and too white!
I like Boo-Berry!
all you need to know about the
controversy between General Mills cereals
and the Spoon Mafia is
that
Cap'n Crunch is not a
real rear-admiral!
he's a Jewish carpenter!
wait, scratch that, I was
responding to the Bumper Sticker Mafia..
okay, no, Jesus was God, but cereal is
good, too!
okay, class!
got that?
take notes!

Cap'n Crunch is definitely not Jewish!
those used to be guys like Sidney and Morty, who
were dentists and gynecologists, good ones!
with warm chests and grey ear hair, but nice!
okay, then, in the 80s, they switched to
being accountants like Woody Allen, named Hebert and Harvey;
no longer good dads
at
all!
and, yes, they also had a couple super tough guy gangsters, like
Meyer Lansky, and Bugsy Seigel, who were called Murder, Inc.
and, well, what happened was, they
left New York and went out west to
found Las Vegas, for
throwing away money to
assuage
white guilt
Boo Berry rocks!
the end...

jerk

collapsing into night's fortress
like a fool
no longer hidden by the dark
a futile cry against the dying of the light
and
the dome of black falling
over the city
helps if you are awake
to witness the spectacle
cause if you aren't, well
nothing's ever gonna mean that much to you
nothing's ever really gonna matter much
which is sad and wrong, this apathy
especially in a land that's struggled so hard
for so many centuries, countless heroes and sheroes
I know that I will never get to be
human
I will never be
a person
I will always be a figure of loss
because I was asleep
for so many of my years
no one can understand
and even if they could, what
is there to really say, but
sorry, sorry kid
tough break
so
I sleep more than half the day

and wonder
what I could've been, would've been
if only I had not been cursed
from birth
with
the walking, talking coma
of my life until
I woke up
too late
to care…

in your all white world

does your chest feel constricted?
do you have a raging migraine?
now, are you so, so sick of trying to figure out how to be happy?
and, okay, do you find yourself tongue-tied, or speechless
all the time?
well, whitey
it's cause you're all white
socially
and
culturally
you feel horrible, and you are almost totally non-verbal
you can't talk right!
that's why
integrate!
culturally, too, don't forget!!

how I wonder where you are

so
leavin' town, are ya?
beatin' it
for
the coast?
LA, I suppose?
LaLa Land…
California dreamin'
you
could
say…
well, I feel ya…
I do, I really do
it's not too surprising, ha ha
this town totally sucks
Winter Falls, Montana
bullshit ass fuckin' city
nothin' good goin' on here
to speak of
at all
nothin' but a bunch a losers all over the place
pissing away their lives
hiding out
hiding out from the real city life
and
the real city people
so
yeah
I don't blame ya

I really don't
not at all
matter of fact
I admire your pluck
you're plucky for that
in my opinion
I hope it works out for ya, kiddo
truly
cause, you know what?
it sure ain't gonna be easy
to make it out there
it really ain't
LA is a huge, huge city
the people are probably alright there
but
it's just an enormous metropolis
to
negotiate
probably gotta go pretty far to get
the stuff you need
and
the stuff you want, too
be careful driving now
and hey
send me
a
postcard
once in a while, baby
and
hey
hey!
make sure don't look up at the sun!
you'll go blind!

ha ha!
have fun, sugarbear!
see ya around!
cool!

what I think President Lincoln should've done...

for real, though?
when The South seceded, all
President Lincoln
should've done was
march his troops down to the top tip of
The Confederacy
and say, even demand
"...okay, you can secede, we
don't mind, we
can cut America in half, and
you are free to have your own country, if
that's what you want
I believe in freedom, and self-determining
nations of people
on their lands
BUT!
BUT!
we know, you are only doing so to
keep on practicing the abhorrent system
of enslaving African-Americans to
work your plantation fields, and
be your butlers, maids, coachmen, etc...
and it's a tragically sad and unmitigatedly painful
and
just horrible, unrelentingly TRAGIC and SAD
life for those African folks
it's a living nightmare, Mr. Davis
that's quite easy to see!

if, you are not stark-raving insane

with

the super-dangerous and super-damaging

so-called "philosophy" of

racism

you can call it bigotry, as well

same thing

so

our bargain with you, which is

non-negotiable

and completely out of your purview to

disagree with; is as follows:

you may secede

and, listen!

you may continue being slave owners, but!

I said, but!

meaning, however!

not

with THESE Africans

not with THESE Africans you have here now

throughout The South

the United States of America

my country

my home

which I am proudly yet humbly leading as

the duly-elected President and Commander-In-Chief of

representing the Republican Party, from

the great city of

Washington, D.C.

is

RESCUING

ALL

THE

AFRICANS
YOU
HAVE
IN
BONDAGE!
TODAY
IN APRIL OF 1861
THAT'S FINAL!
LET THEM COME WITH US UP NORTH
TO LIVE IN FREEDOM AND EQUALITY!!!
ALL OF THEM, DAVIS!
OR
IT'S WAR!
UNFATHOMABLE CARNAGE
WITH NO GOOD MEDICINES OR HEALTH CARE
YET DISCOVERED!
EXCRUTIATING PAIN FOR YOU!
AND YOUR TROOPS!
SAWING OFF LIMBS WITH A SAW WHEN THEY GET
INFECTED
IS WHAT YOU WOULD VISIT ON YOUR COUNTRYMEN
HERE IN YOUR NATION?
TO STOP FREEDOM?
TO FORCE POOR, UNLUCKY, TO SAY THE LEAST
AFRICAN PEOPLE
TO TOIL? ENDLESSLY?
THEY'RE AFRICAN PEOPLE, DAVIS, YOU MONSTER!
THAT'S NOT HARD TO SEE, YOU WICKED IMBECILE!
END OF DEMAND!
THEN, WE WILL BUILD A WALL
ALL ALONG THE MASON-DIXON LINE
AND
YOU ARE FREE

TO
RESTART SLAVERY
IF
YOU
CAN!
BY BUILDING OR BUYING YOUR OWN SLAVE SHIPS
AND
NABBING OR TRADING WITH THE QUEEN OF
ANGOLA
FOR MORE STAR-CROSSED AFRICANS
FROM HER PRISONER OF WAR
RANKS!
THAT'S ALL I HAVE TO SAY, AND
THERE IS NO FURTHER DISCUSSION
NECESSARY!
RELEASE THE REFUGEES!
OR
IT'S
PAIN!
FOR
YOU!
AND
ALL
OF
YOU!!!

oh, Apolonia, girl, if you can hear me, I love you like a major tornado, ah, forget it, I give up...

hello?
is Apolonia home? it's Al..
hold on, I'll get her
APOLONIA!!!
IT'S AL!!!
COMING!!
I GOT IT!
hey
hey, what's up?
not much, just hanging out, you know, reading..
what are you doing?
oh, I was just working on a song
it's a love song
it's about you
oh, God
that's nice
you're sweet, baby..
yeah, I'm thinking about calling it
'I'll never give up on you'
or
'if you only let me'
I got the opening strains, but
the lyrics are gonna take a
few months to
hammer out, to be honest..
wow

that's deep
yeah
thanks
I think I'll play it for you
when it's done
probably at
the
club
you know, 5th Avenue and Manhattan Entrance
one night in April...